MW00891156

Copyright Notice

General Disclaimer

Trevor has a dance coming up and he wants to ask out Sally. He would do anything to go with her and he knows she doesn't have a date. The only problem is that whenever he sees her he gets an extremely large boner. Before he asks her, he practices not getting a boner but nothing works. So he decides to just call her so he doesn't risk a boner. So he calls her and stutters through the words, but she thinks it is cute so she accepts.

At this point he realizes he didn't find a solution to the problem he just put it off. But then he has a great idea! He ties his penis to his leg to conceal the boner. On the day of the dance he heads over to her house and knocks on the door. She answers the door and he kicks her in the face.

■

A husband and wife decide to relive their first date on their 10th anniversary. They come to the fence that they first made love up against. The man looks at his wife "For old time's sake?" She nods and they begin to make love.

He pushes her up against the fence and says "You're even tighter than you were when we started to date!"

She replies "The fence wasn't electric 10 years ago!"

■

A woman wants to find a husband so she puts out an ad "I'm looking for a man that won't hit me, won't run away, and can satisfy me."

A week later she hears a very loud knock at the door. She answers it and it is a man with no arms or legs, he says "I won't beat you, I have no arms. I won't run away, I have no legs."

She replies "And how do you know you can satisfy me?"

He grins and says "Did you hear me knocking?"

■

A pastor is standing before his congregation, "It has come to my attention that somebody has been telling lies about me. Somebody has been saying I am a member of the Ku Klux Klan. This is simply not true! Who has been telling this lie?"

Everybody is silent for a while. He speaks again, "Come on now, face your sins so you can be forgiven!"

Suddenly a drop dead gorgeous blonde rises and says, "I think somebody misunderstood me. I've been telling people that you are a wizard in the sheets."

■

A boy goes to school and he brings his cat. When his teacher asks him why he replies "I heard my dad tell my mom that as soon as I left he was going to eat the p**sy."

■

A man and his wife are setting up the password on their new computer. The man types in 'MyPenis' but the computer denies it. His wife says "I told you it wasn't long enough!"

■

Woman: Can I buy Viagra here?
Pharmacist: Yes.
Woman: Could you give it to me over the counter?
Pharmacist: If you give me two of them, you can.

■

Mrs. Smith, a first grade teacher, is trying to teach her kids how to identify various animals. First is a cheetah so she tells them "This cat has lots of spots." One of the kids guesses "A cheetah!" Next is an elephant so she tells them "This animal is huge and has a trunk." One of the kids says "A elephant!" The final animal is a deer but she can't think of any clues. Finally she tells them "This is what your mommy might call your daddy." One of the kids says "Horny bastard!"

■

Emma didn't get very much sleep last night so she kept falling asleep at Sunday school. While she was sleeping, her teacher decided to ask her a question, "Who created the universe?"

The boy sitting next to her, Joey, poked her with his pencil to help her our. She jumped up and yelled, "God!"

The teacher told her, "Good job!" and continued with the lesson.

Soon after the teacher asked Emma another question, "Who died for our sins?"

Again she is sleeping so Joey pokes her. She wakes up and yells, "Jesus Christ!"

The teacher praises her again and continues.

Not much time passes and the teacher asks Emma, "What did Eve say to Adam after their 26th child?"

Joey pokes her and she yells, "If you put that thing near me again, I'll snap it in half and shove it up your ass!"

■

A man goes to church and tells the priest "Father, I almost cheated on my wife."

The priest asks him "How do you almost cheat on your wife?"

The man says "Well, me and the woman were naked but we just rubbed against each other."

The priest looks at him disgusted and says "Rubbing is the same as putting it in.

Never do it again, say five Hail Mary's and put $100 in the donation pan."

The next time the priest sees the man he is infuriates "You didn't put $100 in the pan!"

The man looks at the priest disgusted and says "I rubbed the money against the pan, and rubbing is the same as putting it in."

■

I ran into a man today who knew absolutely nothing about anatomy. I had to explain to him that their was a vas deferens between a testicle and penis.

■

Q: Why are blonde women always mad when they get their licenses?

A: They get an F in sex.

■

Tom's wife has been in a coma for months. Her attendants have noticed that every time they wash her crotch she moves a little bit. Desperate, they ask Tom if he would perform oral sex on his wife in an attempt to wake her up. Tom agrees and asks for some privacy in the room. Soon after, he rushes out in a panic and says, "I think she's choking!"

■

A man goes to his male doctor after several tests and tells him, "Give it to me straight doc!"

The doctor replies, "That's impossible, we're both male."

They both laugh and the doctor says, "Besides, I don't want HIV"

■

A blonde, a brunette, and a red headed mother are talking about their daughters. The brunette tells them, "I found cigarettes in my daughter's room, I can't believe she smokes!"

4

The read head said "I know, I found some beer in my daughter's room. I couldn't believe it!"

The blonde says "That's nothing! I found condoms in my daughter's room. I never knew she had a penis!"

■

There are 4 types of orgasms: the Holy Orgasm, the Positive Orgasm, the Accidental Orgasm, and the Fake Orgasm.

The Holy Orgasm sounds like, "Oh God! Oh God!"

The Positive Orgasm sounds like, "Oh yes! Oh yes!"

The Accidental Orgasm sounds like, "Oh shit! Oh shit!"

The fake orgasm sounds like, "Oh *INSERT YOUR NAME HERE*!"

■

Q: What is the last thing a Tickle-Me-Elmo gets before he is sent to the stores?
A: Two test tickles!

■

Q: What has six balls and rapes the poor?
A: The lottery.

■

John looked over at his coworker Tom. He noticed that he had an earring on one of his ears. Tom was usually a pretty conservative guy so John is curious. He approached Tom and asked him, "If you don't mind me asking, what's with the earring?"

Tom replied, "Don't worry about it, it's just an earring."

John let it go for a few minutes but then his curiosity peaked again, "So how long have you been wearing and earring?"

Tom replied, "Ever since my wife found it in our bed."

■

A washed up actor hasn't gotten a job in years. He has lost his ability to remember lines. But after looking for work for a very long time, finally he gets the lead role in a Broadway musical.

When he arrives at the theater the director tells him, "You have the most important part, but you only have one line. You walk onto stage with a rose; bring it close to your nose with your thumb, index, and middle fingers; and sniff it deeply. Then you will say, 'Oh, the smell of my lover.'"

When it comes time for him to say his line he walks onto stage and says, "Oh, the smell of my lover." With this the crowd begins to laugh hysterically and the director explodes with anger.

The actor runs off stage and asks, "Did I forget my lines?"

The director replies, "No! You forgot the flower."

■

Q: How are men like spiders?

A: When they are on the web, they always get their hands sticky.

■

There's nothing worse than pooping in an elevator. It really takes shit to a new level.

■

A 90-year-old man goes to the doctor for his annual checkup. The doctor asks him how he is and he replies, "Great, I'm 90 years old, I have an 20 year old bride, and she's pregnant with my child."

The doctor looks at him for a second, "Let me tell you a story. A knew a man who loved to hunt. One day he went out and was in such a hurry he grabbed an umbrella instead of a gun. As soon as he got out there a bear jumped out of the woods at him. He grabbed his umbrella, pointed it at the bear, and squeezed the handle. You know what happened next?"

The old man, dumbfounded, replies, "No, what?"

"The bear dropped dead right there!"

The old man protests, "Someone else must have shot the bear!"

The doctor nods, "Exactly."

■

A guy sleeps with a $5 hooker and gets crabs.

The next day he goes back to complain and the hooker laughs and says, "What did you expect for $5... lobster?"

A man goes to a jewelry store with his girlfriend looking for a wedding ring on Friday. He tells the jeweler, "I need a very special ring for my girlfriend."

The jeweler looks around for a bit and finds a $5,000 ring, "This is a very nice one."

The man yells at the jeweler, "This isn't nearly expensive enough! Get me a better one!"

The jeweler scrambles and finds a $40,000 ring, "How about this one sir?"

The man replies, "That's more like it! I'll write you a check right now. But I know you want to verify I have the funds so I'll pick it up Monday afternoon after you check."

On Monday the jeweler calls the man, "Sir, you don't have nearly enough money in your bank account."

The man replies, "I know, but let me tell you about my weekend!"

■

A man goes to a Japan on business and hires a prostitute for the night. He doesn't speak any Japanese and she barely speaks any English. While they are going at it she yells out, "Gama Su! Gama Su!" Knowing that she has been satisfied he goes to bed.

The next day he plays golf and one of his associates gets a hole in one. Everyone goes crazy, so to enjoy in the excitement he yells, "Gama Su! Gama Su!"

Everybody goes silent and one of his Japanese associates says, "What do you mean wrong hole?"

■

Little Kyle runs into his house one day and immediately confronts his dad, "Dad! I heard these kids at school talking about how awesome a vagina is. What is a vagina, what does it look like?"

The father answers "Well son, before you use it looks like a beautiful flower."

Kyle asks "What about after you use it?"

The father smiles and asks "Have you ever seen a bulldog eating mayonnaise?"

■

Q: How many guys in the friend zone it take to screw in a light bulb?

A: None, they'll just stand around a watch somebody else screw it and complain about it.

■

Mom was cleaning Junior's room one day and she found a bondage magazine under his bed.

This mad he very upset. She put it back under his bed until his father got home and showed him.

He gave it a look and handed it right back to her without a word, so she asked him, 'What should we do about this?'

Dad paused and said, 'Well I don't think you should spank him.'

■

A man and a woman, who are both married to other people, find themselves forced to share a hotel room for a night. They feel weird at first, but they both fall asleep in their separate beds.

After a few hours of sleeping, the man wakes the woman up and asks her, "Could you grab me another blanket from the closet? I'm really cold."

The woman responds, "Or we could just pretend to be married for the night?"

The man replies, "That would be amazing."

The woman smiles and says, "Okay. Get your own fucking blanket!"

■

A man walks up to a house and knocks on the door. A woman answers the door and the man yells "Do you have a vagina?" The woman slams the door in his face. He knocks again and asks the same question, this time she replies "Go away!" This continues for hours.

The woman tells her husband about this and he decides to stay home the next day. Sure enough they see the man coming to the door. The husband hides and his wife answers the door.

The man yells "Do you have a vagina?"

The woman answers: yes.

Then the man tells her "Does your husband know that? Maybe if he did he would stop using my wife's."

■

A guy is going down on his girlfriend and says, "Man you have a big pussy! Man you have a big pussy!"

She snaps back, "Why'd you say it twice?"

He replies, "I didn't..."

Q: What does 80-year-old pussy taste like?

A: Depends…

·

A beautiful blonde woman approaches a pharmacist and asks, "Do you have extra large condoms?"

The pharmacist replies, "Yes, isle 11."

The blonde goes to the isle. But about 30 minutes later she is still looking at the condoms. The pharmacist calls over to her, "Do you need some help?"

The woman replies, "No, I'm just waiting for somebody to buy some."

·

Two hillbillies walk into a bar. They are sitting next to a woman who begins to cough violently. One of the men asks her "Are you okay?" The woman shakes her head no.

He promptly lifts her dress and licks one of her butt cheeks. She instantly spasms violently and spits out the food she was choking on. The hillbilly calmly walks back to his table.

The other man turns to him and says "I've never actually seen somebody use the hind lick maneuver."

·

I was having sex with my girlfriend the other day and she kept yelling some other guy's name. Who the heck is Rape?

·

A few months after his parents were divorced, little Johnny passed by his mom's bedroom and saw her rubbing her body and moaning, "I need a man, I need a man!".

Over the next couple of months, he saw her doing this several times.

One day, he came home from school and heard her moaning. When he peeked into her bedroom, he saw a man on top of her. Little Johnny ran into his room, took off his clothes, threw himself on his bed, started stroking himself, and moaning, "Oh, I need a bike! I need a bike!"

·

I know a black guy that is dating a white chick that swears he has never eaten a cracker.

Q: What do you call a gay male dinosaur?

A: A Mega-saur-ass.

■

Nena: Grandma, we played high jump & tumbling at school.

Grandma: What? How many times do I have to tell you not to play that kind of game because your schoolmates will see your underwear.

Nena: Oh don't worry Grandma, because this time I already took off my panties and put in in my bag ..

■

Q: Have you seen the new movie Constipated?

A: Ittttttt hasn'ttttt commmmme ooooout yeeeeet!

■

Teacher: "Johnny, write a sentence ending with the word hand."

Johnny: "My penis in your hand."

Teacher: "What?"

Johnny: "Sorry teacher, I forgot to put a space between pen is."

■

Little Johnny asks his mother how old she is.

Her reply is, "Gentlemen don't ask ladies that question."

Johnny then asks his mother how much she weighs.

Again the mother's reply is, "Gentlemen don't ask ladies that question."

The boy then asks, "Why did daddy leave you?"

To this, the mother says, "you shouldn't ask that" and then sends him to his room.

On the way to his room, the boy trips over his mother's purse. When he picks it up, her driver's license falls out. The boy looks it over and goes back to his mother saying, "I know all about you now. You are 36 years old, weigh 127 pounds and daddy left you because you got an 'F' in sex!"

■

Little Johnny walks in on his parents having sex and asks, "What are you doing?"

His father says, "We're playing cards, and your mother is my wild card."

A week later, Little Johnny walks in on his father masturbating.

He asks, "What are you doing?"

His father says, "I'm playing cards." "Where's your wild card?"

Johnny asks. His father replies, "Son, you don't need one when you've got a good hand."

∎

The teacher asked little Johnny, "What's two and two?".

He counted 1-2-3-4 on his fingers and said, "Four, teacher?".

She said, " Yes, that's right, but you counted on your fingers. Put your hands behind behind your back and tell me what's three and three".

He put his hands behind his back, fumbled around, and answered, "Six, teacher?".

She said, "Yes, that's right, but you're still counting on your fingers.

Put your hands in your pockets and tell me what's five and five".

He put his hands in his pockets, fumbled around, and replied, "Eleven, teacher?".

∎

An old man on crowded bus has trouble finding a seat. The bus careened down the avenue, shaking the passengers from left to right, and the old man, unable to support himself properly with his cane, fell to the floor.

Little Johnny, sitting nearby, looked down at him and said, "If you put a little rubber cap on the end of your cane, you wouldn't fall like that.

The old man looked up and replied, "If your daddy had done the same, I would have a place to sit on this stupid bus.

∎

One night Little Johnny was really scared sleeping by himself at camp, so he sprints out of his tent and runs to his teachers tent and asks: "Miss can I please sleep with you tonight ?".

His teacher replies: "NO" ,

Johnny moans and says: "But my mummy lets me".

"OK then, just for tonight" the teacher replies.

Johnny jumps into bed with her and asks: "Miss can I please play with your belly button with my finger".

She again says: "NO".

"But my mummy lets me", says Johnny again.

"Well I suppose it's OK", replies the teacher. Things are silent for a few minutes until the teacher leaps up screaming: "THAT'S NOT MY BELLY BUTTON"

Little Johnny replies: "It is not my finger either".

■

One day, Little Johnny overheard his parents fighting. Later, he asked what "bitch" and "bastard" mean. They explained that they mean "lady" and "gentleman." The next day, he overheard his parents having sex. He later asked what "penis" and "vagina" mean. His parents explained that they refer to "hats" and "coats." At supper the next day, Little Johnny's mom cut her finger in the kitchen and yelled, "Oh f**k!" Little Johnny asked what that meant, and she said it means "cut." A week later, guests arrive for Thanksgiving dinner. Little Johnny welcomes them at the door, saying, "Hello bitches and bastards! Hurry up with your penises and vaginas we can't wait to f**k the turkey!"

■

There was this little boy who had no name. One day he went outside and heard someone say Jonny. He then tells his mother his first name would be Jonny.

The second day he goes outside and hears the name Humper. So, he tells his mother his middle name was going to be Humper.

The third day, Jonny goes out and hears the name Harder. Then, he tells his mother his full name shall be Jonny Humper Harder.

Jonny goes out one day with handful of cookies. He sees this girl around his age and asks her if she would be willing to take off her shirt for a cookie. The little girls says that she would take off all her clothes for all of Jonny's cookies. Jonny gives her the cookies and the girl takes off all her clothes. Hours later, the town's people all run up to them in the middle of the street and they cry, "JONNY HUMPER HARDER!"

Little Jonny yells, "I'M TRYING, I'M TRYING!"

■

Little Johnny catches his parents going at it.

He says, "Hey, Dad! What are you doing?"

His father says, "I'm filling your mother's tank."

Johnny says, "Oh, yeah? Well, you should get a model that gets better mileage. The milkman filled her this morning."

■

Little Johnny asks, "Mommy, where do babies come from?"

His mother replies, "The stork brings them."

Little Johnny, puzzled, asks, "Then who fucks the stork?"

■

While playing in the backyard, Little Johnny kills a honeybee.

His father sees him killing the honeybee and angrily says, "No honey for you for one month!".

Later that afternoon, Johnny's dad catches him tearing the wings off a butterfly. "That's it! No butter for you for one month!", says his dad.

Later that evening as Johnny's mother cooks dinner, a cockroach run across the kitchen floor. She jumps and stomps on it, and then looks up to find Little Johnny and her husband watching her.

Little Johnny looks at his father and says, "Are you going to tell her, Dad, or do you want me to?"

■

A teacher asks her class, "What do you want to be when you grow up?".

Little Johnny says: "I wanna be a billionaire, going to the most expensive clubs, take the best bitch with me, give her a Ferrari worth over a million bucks, an apartment in Hawaii, a mansion in Paris, a jet to travel through Europe, an Infinite Visa Card and to make love to her three times a day".

The teacher, shocked, and not knowing what to do with the bad behavior of the child, decides not to give importance to what he said and then continues the lesson.

"And you, Susie? " the teacher asks.

Susie says "I wanna be Johnny's bitch."

■

A Concerned mother warns her little boy, "don't look at naked women or you'll turn to stone."

Johnny loved his mother, and as such decided not to look at naked women.

But one day Johnny and his friend were walking along a beach, and saw a woman sunbathing naked. Johnny remembered what his mother said, and turned and ran away from the woman, his friend finally catches up to him and asks why he ran.

Johnny told his friend what his mother said, and then added, "and it must be true, because when I saw that woman I felt myself going rock hard in my trousers.

■

Fred and Mary got married, but can't afford a honeymoon, so they go back to Fred's parent's home for their first night together. In the morning, Johnny, Fred's little brother, gets up and has his breakfast. As he is going out of the door to go to school, he asks his Mom if Fred and Mary are up yet.

She replies, "No".

Johnny asks, "Do you know what I think?"

His mom replies, "I don't want to hear what you think! Just go to school."

Johnny comes home for lunch and asks his mom, "Are Fred and Mary up yet?"

She replies, "No."

Johnny says, "Do you know what I think?"

His mom replies, "Never mind what you think! Eat your lunch and go back to school."

After school, Johnny comes home and asks again, "Are Fred and Mary up yet?"

His mom says "No." He asks, "Do you know what I think?"

His Mom replies, "Ok, do tell me what you think?"

He says: "Last night Fred came to my room for the Vaseline and I think I gave him my airplane glue."

■

Little Johnny attended a horse auction with his father. He watched as his father moved from horse to horse, running his hands up and down the horse's legs and rump, and chest.

After a few minutes, Johnny asked, "Dad, why are you doing that?"

His father replied, "Because when I'm buying horses, I have to make sure that they are healthy and in good shape before I buy.

Johnny, looking worried, said, "Dad, I think the UPS guy wants to buy Mom."

·

A teacher was teaching her second grade class about the government, so for homework that one day, she told her students to ask their parents what the government is.

When Little Johnny got home that day, he went up to his dad and ask his what the government was.

His dad thought for a while and answered, "Look at it this way: I'm the president, your mom is Congress, your maid is the work force, you are the people and your baby brother is the future."

"I still don't get it" responded the Little Johnny.

"Why don't you sleep on it then? Maybe you'll understand it better," said the dad.

"Okay then...good night", said Little Jonny went off to bed. In the middle of the night, Little Johnny was awakened by his baby brother's crying. He went to his baby brother's crib and found that his baby brother had taken a crap in his diaper. So Little Johnny went to his parent's room to get help. When he got to his parent's bedroom, he looked through the keyhole to check if his parents were asleep. Through the keyhole he saw his mom loudly snoring, but this dad wasn't there. So he went to the maid's room. When he looked through the maid's room keyhole, he saw his dad having sex with his maid. Little Johnny was surprised, but then he just realized some thing and thinks aloud, "OH!! Now I understand the government! The President is screwing the work force, Congress is fast asleep, nobody cares about the people, and the future is full of shit!"

·

One day, Little Johnny saw his grandpa smoking his cigarettes. Little Johnny asked, "Grandpa, can I smoke some of your cigarettes?"

His grandpa replied, "Can your penis reach your asshole?"

"No", said Little Johnny.

His grandpa replied, "Then you're not old enough."

The next day, Little Johnny saw his grandpa drinking beer. He asked, "Grandpa, can I drink some of your beer?"

His grandpa replied, "Can your penis reach your asshole?"

"No" said Little Johnny. "Then you're not old enough." his grandpa replied. The next day, Little Johnny was eating cookies.

His grandpa asked, "Can I have some of your cookies?"

Little Johnny replied, "Can your penis reach your asshole?" His grandpa replied, "It most certainly can!"

Little Johnny replied, "Then go fuck yourself.

■

So Little Johnny's teacher is warned at the beginning of the school year not to ever make a bet with Johnny unless she is absolutely sure she will win it. One day in class, Johnny raises his hand and says "teacher, I'll bet you $50 I can guess what color your underwear is."

She replies, "okay, meet me after class and we'll settle it."

But before class ends, she goes to the restroom and removes her panties. After class is over and the students clear out, Johnny makes his guess. "Blue."

"Nope. You got it wrong," she says as she lifts her skirt to reveal she isn't wearing any underwear.

"Well come with me out to my dad's car, he's waiting for me, and I'll get you the money." She follows him out. When they get to the car she informs his dad that he got the bet wrong and that she showed Johnny that she wasn't wearing any underwear. His dad exclaims: "That mother fucker! He bet me $100 this morning that he'd see your pussy before the end of the day!"

■

A teacher was working with a group of children, trying to broaden their horizons through sensory perception. She brought in a variety of lifesavers and said, "Children, I'd like you to close your eyes and taste these."

The kids easily identified the taste of cherries, lemons and mint, but when the teacher gave them honey-flavored lifesavers, all of the kids were stumped.

"I'll give you a hint," said the teacher. "It's something your mommy probably calls your daddy all the time."

Instantly, Little Johnny coughed his onto the floor and shouted, "Quick! Spit'em out! They're assholes!"

■

Little Johnny comes home from sunday school with a black eye. His father sees it and says, "Johnny, how many times do I have to tell you not to fight with the other boys?",

"But Dad, it wasn't my fault. We were all in church saying our prayers. We all stood up and my teacher in front of me had her dress in the crack of her butt. I reached over and pulled it out. That's when she hit me!"

"Johnny," the father said. "You don't do those kind of things to women."

Sure enough, the very next sunday Johnny came home with the other eye black and blue. Johnny's father said, "Johnny, I thought we had a talk!"

"But Dad," Johnny said, "It wasn't my fault. There we were in church saying our prayers. We all stood up and my teacher in front of us had her dress in the crack of her butt. Then Louie who was sitting next to me saw it and he reached over and pulled it out. Now I know she doesn't like this, so I pushed it back in!"

■

Joe Bob goes to Billy Bob's barn to see what he's been up to. He sees Billy stripping for his John Deere tractor. He slowly removes his overalls and twerks on it. Joe bursts in and asks, "Billy! What are you doing?"

Billy exclaims, "Dang Joe! You scared the life out of me! Me and the wife went to counseling and the therapist says I need to do something sexy to a tractor."

■

A man kills a deer and takes it home to cook for dinner. Both he and his wife decide that they won't tell the kids what kind of meat it is, but will give them a clue and let them guess. The dad said, "Well it's what Mommy calls me sometimes."

The little girl screamed to her brother, "Don't eat it. It's an asshole!

■

There once was a boy who really had to fart. He came up with a plan. He would drop his textbook and fart at the same time. He dropped his book and everyone stared at him. He then farted.

■

The teacher asked Jimmy, "Why is your cat at school today Jimmy?"

Jimmy replied crying, "Because I heard my daddy tell my mommy, 'I am going to eat that p*ssy once Jimmy leaves for school today!'"

■

A man and his wife were having financial troubles so they decide she should work the streets to make some extra money.

She comes home that night with $31.25. He asks her, "Who the hell gave you a quarter?"

She replies, "All of them."

■

A blonde woman wants to bath in milk because she heard it makes your skin silky smooth. So when the milkman comes she tells him "I'm going to need 25 gallons of milk."

He replies "Damn, what for?"

She tells him "I want to bath in it."

Confused he asks her "Would you like that pasteurized?"

She replies "No, just up to my tits is fine. I'll splash it on my eyes."

∎

A blonde man and blonde woman are watching TV and they see that a particular tribe in Africa ties weights around their penis' to make them grow up to 24 inches long. The woman tells the husband that they should do it and he agrees.

The next day she asks him how it is going and he tells her "Half way there."

She asks him "It's 12 inches long?!"

He replies "Nope. But it's black."

∎

A man and his wife are on their honeymoon. To show his dominance, the man takes off his pants and tells the woman, "Put on my pants."

She does but she says, "They're too big, they don't fit me."

He responds, "That's right, that's why I wear the pants in the relationship and always will."

The woman tells the man to put on her underwear. He tries but can't. He says, "I can't get into your panties."

She replies, "That's the way it's going to be unless you stop being an asshole."

∎

A man from Tennessee takes his daughter to the doctor and tells the doctor his daughter need birth control.

The doctor asks, "How old is she?"

He replies, "15."

"And she's sexually active," the doctor asks.

The man replies, "Naw, she just lays there like her mother."

∎

Tom and Sally decided to have a little Sunday quickie but had to figure out what to do with their 10-year-old son since they lived in a small apartment. They

18

cleverly sent him out on the balcony and had him report all of the neighborhood activities.

The boy began his commentary as his parents put their plan into action. "There's a car being towed from the parking lot," he said. "An ambulance just drove by." A few moments passed. "Looks like the Anderson's have company," he called out. "Matt's riding a new bike and the Coopers are having sex."

Mom and dad shot up in bed. "How do you know that?" the startled father asked.

"Their kid is waving at me from their balcony."

■

A man who smelled like a distillery flopped on a subway seat next to a priest. The man's tie was stained, his face was plastered with red lipstick, and a half empty bottle of gin was sticking out of his torn coat pocket. He opened his newspaper and began reading. After a few minutes, the disheveled man turned to the priest and asked, "Say, Father, what causes arthritis?"

The priest replied "Mister, it's caused by loose living, being with cheap women, too much alcohol and a contempt for your fellow man."

"Well I'll be," the drunk muttered, returning to his paper.

The priest, thinking about what he had said, nudged the man and apologized, "I'm very sorry. I didn't mean to come on so strong. How long have you had arthritis?"

"I don't have it Father. I was just reading here that the Pope does."

■

A man and his wife have a big argument. She yells at him and tells him to get out.

He grabs his stuff and starts to walk out the door and she yells to him, "I hope you have a slow painful death bastard!"

He yells back to her, "Now you want me to stay?!"

■

What is hairy on the outside, wet and fleshy on the inside, starts with C and ends with T, and has a U and N in the middle?

■

Johnny came to school with a black eye so his teacher asked him what had happened. He told her, "My family doesn't have any money, so me, my mom, and my

19

dad all share a bed. My dad asked me if I was asleep yet and I told him no, so he hit me."

His teacher told him, "Tonight when you go to bed, if your dad asks you if you're awake just pretend to be asleep."

The next day Johnny came in with two black eyes. His teacher, appalled, asks him what happened. Johnny replies, "So I did what you said. Then the bed started shaking and my mom was yelling and my dad was grunting. After a while my mom yelled, 'I'm coming! Are you coming!' Then he yelled back that he was coming. But my parents never go anywhere without me, so I yelled, 'Wait for me, I'm coming too!'"

■

Mr. Daniels is diagnosed with a rare disease and he only has about 12 hours left to live. His wife begins to cry and tells him that she will give him a night to remember.

Shortly after making love for the first time his wife says "Do you want to go again?" This time it is even better than the first time.

Mrs. Daniels starts to doze off so Mr. Daniels nudges her and asks if they can do it one final time. Mrs. Daniels replies "Easy for you to say, you don't have to get up in the morning."

■

Two nuns are taking a walk when they are attacked by vampires. One of the nuns yells "Sister Annie! Show them your cross!"

Sister Annie runs at the vampires and yells "Get the fuck out of here!"

■

Sally has been feeling harassed by one of her coworkers, John. She tells her employer that he has been harassing her and he asks her, "What does he do?"

She says, "He always tells me my hair smells nice."

Her boss replies, "That's not really sexual harassment."

Sally says, "He's three feet tall."

■

A pastor is standing before his congregation, "It has come to my attention that somebody has been telling lies about me. Somebody has been saying I am a member of the Ku Klux Klan. This is simply not true! Who has been telling this lie?"

Everybody is silent for a while. He speaks again, "Come on now, face your sins so you can be forgiven!"

Suddenly a drop dead gorgeous blonde rises and says, "I think somebody misunderstood me. I've been telling people that you are a wizard in the sheets."

■

Little Timmy is walking home from the park and pulling his little red wagon up a hill. As he is getting tired he says "Damn. Fuck this shit."

A nun from the church nearby tells him "Little Timmy! You shouldn't swear like that. God is everywhere and always watching you."

"So he is up in the clouds and in the church?" asks little Timmy.

"Exactly," replied the nun.

Timmy asks "And in my wagon?"

The nun replies "Yes child."

Timmy is suddenly enraged "Well tell him to get his lazy ass out and push!"

■

A man goes to a Japan on business and hires a prostitute for the night. He doesn't speak any Japanese and she barely speaks any English. While they are going at it she yells out, "Gama Su! Gama Su!" Knowing that she has been satisfied he goes to bed.

The next day he plays golf and one of his associates gets a hole in one. Everyone goes crazy, so to enjoy in the excitement he yells, "Gama Su! Gama Su!"

Everybody goes silent and one of his Japanese associates says, "What do you mean wrong hole?"

■

A little girl and boy are in a doctor's waiting room waiting for the doctor. The little girl starts to cry so the little boy asks her "What's wrong?"

The little girl responds "I have to get a blood test so they're going to cut open my finger."

The little boy's jaw drops and he says "Oh no! I'm getting a urine test."

■

Tom and John are hanging out. Tom asks John, "It's fuckin' freezin' in here. Can you get me my fuckin' slippers?"

John goes upstairs to get the slippers and he comes across Tom's hot 21-year-old twin sisters. He tells them, "Your brother told me to have sex with both of you."

One of the sisters replies, "Prove it!"

John yells downstairs, "Tom! Both of them?!."

Tom yells back, "Of course! What's the point of fuckin' one?!."

·

A man invents a machine that slaps anybody who lies. He tries it out on his family at dinner. He asks his son, "Why were you so late last night getting home?"

The son replies, "I was just studying at the library." *SLAP!* "Fine, I was at John's house watching TV." *SLAP!* "Fine, porn!"

His father looks at him disgusted, "At your age I didn't even know what porn was." *SLAP!*

The man's wife begins to laugh, "He's definitely your son." *SLAP!*

·

Mom was cleaning Junior's room one day and she found a bondage magazine under his bed.

This mad he very upset. She put it back under his bed until his father got home and showed him.

He gave it a look and handed it right back to her without a word, so she asked him, 'What should we do about this?'

Dad paused and said, 'Well I don't think you should spank him.'

·

Tyler and Connor have a friend named Nico. They like everything about him except the fact that he is extremely optimistic and always sees the bright side of everything. So one day they decide to tell him a story that he cannot find the positive in.

Nico meets Tyler at his house and Nico asks where Connor is. Tyler tells him "You didn't hear? He found his girlfriend with another guy last night and killed them both then he killed himself."

Nico says "Thank God!"

Tyler looks at him and says "Are you serious?"

Nico says "Yeah, if that would have happened a few nights ago I would be dead."

·

A man walks into the bank and walks up to the teller. She asks him "Can I help you sir?"

The man replies "Yeah, I want to open up a fucking bank account."

She tells him "Sir, we don't tolerate that sort of language here." She then gets the manager, who agrees that she should not put up with the man's language.

The manager approaches the man and asks "Sir, do we have an issue here?"

The man replies "No! I just want to put this motherfucking 100 million dollars I won in the goddamn lottery into a bank account."

"Oh," says the manager, "was this bitch giving you trouble, sir?"

■

A man goes to an assassin because his wife is sleeping with his best friend. The assassin tells him, "It's going to cost you $1000 per bullet."

The man says, "What if you miss?"

The assassin replies, "I don't miss."

With this they head off to the motel where his wife is with his friend. The man says, "I want my wife shot in the head and I want you to blow my friends dick off."

The assassin takes aim and waits a few minutes, "Aren't you going to shoot?"

The assassin replies, "Hold up, I think I can save you $1000."

■

A doctor told a man, "You're going to have to stop masturbating."
The man asked him "Why?"
The doctor replied "It is extremely distracting."

■

A man with a penis that was 25 inches long went to a witch to see if she could reduce its size. She told him "Go to the forest. There you will find a toad. Ask it to marry you."

So the man went into the forest and found the toad she spoke of. He asked the toad if it would marry him and the toad responded "No." Instantly his penis shrunk by 5 inches.

He asked again and the toad again responded "No!" His penis went down to 15 inches in size. He realized that whenever the toad said no to him, his penis would shrink 5 inches.

Figuring that 15 inches was still to big he decided to ask the toad one final time. The toad responded "Are you deaf? How many times do I have to say it? No! No! No!"

23

Mrs. Smith: "Why do you think you deserve a raise?"
Maid: "I have three reasons. The first is that I cook better than you."
Mrs. Smith: "Who told you that?"
Maid: "Your husband did. The second reason is that I clean better than you do."
Mrs. Smith: "Who told you that?"
Maid: "Your husband did. The final reason is that I am better in bed than you are."
Mrs. Smith: "I suppose my husband said that too?!"
Maid: "No, the gardener."
Mrs. Smith: "How much do you want?"

■

A man comes home early from work one day and finds his wife naked in bed. He turns and sees a man's feet coming from the curtains. Angry he goes over and pulls the curtains away saying "Who the hell are you?"

The man replies "Why I'm the moth exterminator."

The husband asks "Why are you naked?"

The man replies "Oh my god. I'm too late!"

■

A woman gets onto a bus and sits in front of a couple of Italian gentlemen. They talk very loudly but she ignores it. But a few minutes later she hears one of them say, "Emma comes first. Then I come. Then two asses come together. I come once-a-more. Two asses come together again. I come again then pee twice. Then I come one last-a-time."

With this the lady turns around and says, "Excuse me! You perverts shouldn't be talking about sex on a bus."

One of them turns around and says, "Whose talking abouta sex? I'm justa teaching him how to spell 'Mississippi'."

■

Little Timmy is walking home from the park and pulling his little red wagon up a hill. As he is getting tired he says "Damn. Fuck this shit."

A nun from the church nearby tells him "Little Timmy! You shouldn't swear like that. God is everywhere and always watching you."

"So he is up in the clouds and in the church?" asks little Timmy.

"Exactly," replied the nun.

Timmy asks "And in my wagon?"

The nun replies "Yes child."

Timmy is suddenly enraged "Well tell him to get his lazy ass out and push!"

■

Three men are captured and are going to be killed. The only way they can live is if they pass a trial. They must go into the jungle and find ten pieces of fruit.

The first man comes back quickly with ten apples. The leader of the men who captured them then says, "Now you must shove them up your ass without facial expression."

The man puts the first apple up there with no problem. But on the second apple he winces and is killed.

The next man comes back with some small berries. They tell him the same thing. Suddenly, while he is putting the tenth berry up there he bursts into laughter.

The first man and the second man meet in heaven. The first man asks, "You were so close, why did you laugh?"

He replies, "I saw the last guy returning with pineapples."

■

One day a wife asked her husband, "Honey, would you please mow the lawn?" Her husband responded "Who do you think I am, John Deer?"

Later the wife asked, "Would you please paint the house?" Her husband said, "Who do you think I am, Sherwin Williams?" Then he left to go fishing for the weekend.

When he got back home, he was surprised to see the lawn was mowed and the house was painted. He asked her how she got all of it done. She said, "The guy next door did it. He wanted me to either bake him a cake or give him a blow job."

So the husband asked, "What kind of cake did you bake?" She replied, "Who do you think I am, Betty Crocker?"

■

A little boy catches his dad looking at porn and asks him "Dad, what's that between the guys legs?"

The father responds "That's his third leg."

25

Then the little boy asks "What about that lady?"

The father replies "Well that's her second mouth."

The little boy thinks for a while and says "Is that why guys walk so fast and women talk so much?"

■

A bunch of nuns die in a freak accident. When they arrive to heaven they meet Saint Peter at the pearly gates. The first nun approaches him.

"Sister, have you ever touched a penis?" he asked.

The nun blushes and says "Well, once I touched one. But just with my finger tip."

Saint Peter says "Just dip your finger tips in the holy water and all will be forgiven." He asks the next nun the same question.

She replies giggling "Well, I gave a man a hand job once."

"Just dip your hands into the holy water and all will be forgiven," he says again.

Suddenly there is a lot of movement among the nuns. "What is going on?" Saint Peter asks.

One nun comes forward and says "If I'm going to have to gargle the holy water I'm doing it before Sister Mary dips her ass in it!"

■

■

A man's wife is standing in front of a mirror naked and says "Look at me. I'm fat, wrinkly, and old. Is there anything still good about me honey?"

Her husband responds "You have great eyesight!"

■

A man has a girlfriend named Wendy so he gets her name tattooed on his penis. When his penis is erect it reads, "WENDY," but when it's flaccid it just reads, "WY."

While at a restaurant he goes to the bathroom next to a large Jamaican man. He looks over and notices "WY" on the mans penis. So he asks him, "You have a girlfriend named Wendy too?"

The man replies, "No man. It says, 'Welcome to Jamaica, have a nice day'."

■

A blonde girl comes home from school one day and tells her mom "We were learning our numbers today and everyone else could only count to 5, I could count to 10. 1, 2, 3, 4, 5, 6, 7, 8, 9, 10!"

Her mom tells her "Great job honey!"

The girl asks her mom "Is it because I'm blonde?" Her mom tells her it is.

The next day the blonde girl comes home from school and tells her mom "We were learning our alphabets today and everyone else could only get to E, I got to J. A, B, C, D, E, F, G, H, I, J!"

Her mom tells her "Great job honey!"

The girl asks her mom "Is it because I'm blonde?" Her mom tells her it is.

The blonde girl comes home from school the next day and tells her mom "Today we were in the showers after gym class and all of the other girls were flat chested, and I have these!" The girl lifts her shirt revealing very large breasts.

Her mom tells her "Um... Great job honey."

The girl asks her mom "Is it because I'm blonde?"

Her mom replies "No dear, it's because you're 25."

∎

A guy moves into a new house just outside of the city. While he is unpacking his car a truck pulls up and the window rolls down "Hey there neighbor! I just saw you were moving in and I wanted to invite you to a welcome party."

The guy puts his box down and replies "That sounds great."

The guy gets out of his truck and says "Yeah, there will be drinking, fighting, dancing and sex."

The new guy replies "Oh, okay. What should I wear?"

"You look fine," the neighbor replies, "It's just gonna be me and you anyways."

∎

A prostitute is on the job for the first day. Trying to make friends, she asks the prostitute next to her, "Have you ever been picked up by the fuzz?"

The other woman replies, "Nope. But I was swung by my tits once!"

∎

A man is walking down the road and another man runs up to him and asks him, "Do you want to see my talking ducks?"

The man, not wanting to be rude, decides to take a look.

When they arrive at the farm the man looks at one of the ducks and asks, "Hey little buddy, how's your day going?"

The duck replies, "Pretty good, I've just been in and out of puddles all day."

The man is amazed by the talking duck and asks the next one how his day has been. The duck replies, "Pretty good, I've just been in and out of puddles all day."

Stunned, the man asks a third duck the same question. The duck replies, "Shitty."

The man asks him, "Why is that?"

The duck replies, "I'm puddles."

■

A man walks up to a large woman on a table and says "Damn! Nice legs."

She replies "You really think so?"

The man says "Hell yeah! Most tables would have broken by now. Must be oak."

■

Three strangers are sitting at a bar quietly. One of the men goes to the bathroom and the two remaining men start to talk "How's life?"

The other man says "Pretty good, I just got promoted and bought my girlfriend a Mercedes. How about you?"

The other man replies "No complaints. Me and my girlfriend just got a house down in California."

The third man comes back from the bathroom with a grin on his face. The other men ask him why he is so happy and he says "My girlfriend just called me and said she is taking me to California for the weekend in her new Mercedes!"

■

A man goes to a restaurant where he sees a sign on the wall that says: "If we can't fill your order, we'll give you $500."

So when the waitress comes to his table he orders, "I'll have rye toast with elephant dung."

The waitress writes down his order and calmly walks to the kitchen. About ten minutes later the manager storms out of the kitchen and lays out $500 on the man's table. Angry, the manager says, "Are you happy? This is the first time in ten years we haven't had rye bread!"

■

A very religious woman has a parrot that prays. He sits at the bottom of his cage whispering prayers all day. She brags about her bird to everyone she meets.

One day she is bragging and a man says that he has a female parrot who is always swearing. They decide that it would be a good idea to put them together so the female parrot can learn from the praying male parrot.

So the man brings his female parrot over and they put her in the cage. The male parrot looks up at her from his prayer and says "Thank Jesus! My prayers have been answered!"

■

A man is checking into a hotel with his family and whispers to the clerk, "I hope the porn channels are disabled."

The clerk whispered back, "Nope, it's just regular porn you sick bastard."

■

A guy walks into a bar and approaches another man at the counter and says, "I just fucked your mother. We did it in your bed and I came all over her. What do you think about that?"

The other guy replies, "Dad, you're drunk."

■

A man takes a job as the cook on a ship just before a long voyage. He looks around the kitchen for a few hours and all he can find is potatoes in the shape of penises.

He finds the captain and asks him, "Captain, what's with all of the penis shaped potatoes? That's all I can find and I don't think I like it."

The captain looks at him sternly and says, "There's nothing you can do about it. This is a dictatorship!"

■

A girl hears about her grandfather dying so she goes to visit her grandmother. When she gets to her grandma's house she asks her what had happened. Her grandma replies "We were making love on a Sunday morning and he had a heart attack."

The girl is shocked, "Grandma, at your age sex is probably never a good idea."

Her grandmother replies "Don't worry dear. Your grandfather and I figured out a safe way. Every Sunday we would make love to the sound of the church bells, they were the perfect rhythm. If it wasn't for the ice cream truck, he would still be alive."

■

A man and his pregnant wife go to the doctor because she has started labor. When they arrive the doctor tells them of a great new invention he has made. He made a machine that can transfer pain from the mother to the father. The couple is ecstatic and quickly agrees, but the doctor warns the man, "Even 10% of the pain is probably more pain than you've ever felt."

They start at 10% and the husband is not effected at all. He insists they move it up to 50%. He is still not phased by the pain, but his wife is feeling a lot better. So he tells the doctor to give him all of the pain. The woman has her baby with no pain and they are all very happy.

When they get home the UPS man is dead on the porch.

■

My friend and I were sitting at the bar and saw some old and sad looking drunks. I laughed and said "That's us in twenty years."

My friend slapped me and said "That's a mirror, dumbass."

■

A man went to the doctor because he could no longer get an erection. The doctor told him to bring his wife in. So the next day the man comes in with his wife. First, the doctor tells her, "Take off all of your clothes." So she does.

Next he tells her, "Now turn around... Okay, good. Now lie down." With this he pulls the man aside and tells him, "You are perfectly healthy. I didn't get a boner either."

■

Tom's wife has been in a coma for months. Her attendants have noticed that every time they wash her crotch she moves a little bit. Desperate, they ask Tom if he would perform oral sex on his wife in an attempt to wake her up. Tom agrees and asks for some privacy in the room. Soon after, he rushes out in a panic and says, "I think she's choking!"

■

A washed up actor hasn't gotten a job in years. He has lost his ability to remember lines. But after looking for work for a very long time, finally he gets the lead role in a Broadway musical.

When he arrives at the theater the director tells him, "You have the most important part, but you only have one line. You walk onto stage with a rose; bring it close to your nose with your thumb, index, and middle fingers; and sniff it deeply. Then you will say, 'Oh, the smell of my lover."

When it comes time for him to say his line he walks onto stage and says, "Oh, the smell of my lover." With this the crowd begins to laugh hysterically and the director explodes with anger.

The actor runs off stage and asks, "Did I forget my lines?"

The director replies, "No! You forgot the flower."

■

Three guys are hanging out at one of their houses when a terrible storm starts. It's so bad that they can't leave the house all night. So they decide to go to bed, the only problem is that there is only one large bed so they all have to share it.

When they wake up the next morning the guy who slept on the right says, "I had the best dream, a beautiful woman was giving me a handjob."

Next the guy who slept on the left side says, "That's weird, I had a dream where I was getting a handjob from a sexy lady."

The last guy, the one in the middle, frowns and says, "I had a dream I was skiing."

■

A prostitute is at a man's house after accepting payment. The man is in the bathroom taking a shower when the woman realizes she is on her period. She already accepted payment and the man is attractive, so she decides to turn the lights off and leave early in the morning.

They have some wild drunkin' sex and the woman leaves early in the morning. When the guy wakes up he sees a pool of blood next to him in the bed. "I must have shot her," he thinks to himself. But when he checks his gun it hasn't been shot.

Then he thinks, "I must have stabbed her." But when he checks the knifes in the kitchen their is not blood.

At this point he goes to the bathroom and looks up at himself in the mirror, "Oh no! I ate her!"

■

One day a priest leaves the church and decides to sit at a nearby pier and watch the fisherman. While sitting, one of the fisherman invites the priest to join him. The priest agrees and they start fishing. After a few minutes the priest pulls up a huge fish. The priest, shocked, yells out, "Woah! Look at that son of a bitch!"

The priest looks at the fisherman and says, "Please mind your language."

The fisherman replies, "Oh... No father, that's the name of a fish. It's a son of a bitch."

The priest heads back to the church. On his way he sees the bishop and addresses him, "Look at the son of a bitch I just caught at the pier!"

The bishop replies, "Father! You are in the house of the lord!"

The priest says, "Oh no! That's the name of the fish, it's a son of a bitch."

The bishop replies, "Oh, if you give me it I can clean it and have Mother Superior cook it for our dinner with the pope."

He cleans the fish and brings it to Mother Superior, "Can you cook this son of a bitch."

She replies, "Why I never! What language for a bishop!"

The bishop tells her, "No, that's the name of the fish. Can you cook it for our dinner with the pope?"

She agrees and makes it up for their dinner with the pope. They sit down with the pope and he takes one bite, "This is wonderful! What is it?"

The priest says, "I caught that son of a bitch."

The bishop says, "I cleaned that son of a bitch."

Mother Superior says, "And I cooks that son of a bitch."

The pope gives them all a blank stare for a moment, takes off his hat, puts it on the table, and says, "You fuckers are alright."

■

A lady cop pulls over an old man and his wife. She asks the man for his license and registration. He asks his wife, "What did she say?"

His wife replies, "She asked for your license and registration dear." He hands the officer what she asked for.

The police woman then says, "Oh you're from New York? I used to have a lover from New York. But he was a terrible lover."

The man asks his wife, "What did she say?"

His wife replies, "She thinks she used to know you."

■

Lisa's mom is doing laundry and Lisa brings in a shirt and says "I've got another dirty shirt."

Her mother who is hard of hearing replies "Come again?"

Surprised Lisa says "No, paint."

■

A man who smelled like a distillery flopped on a subway seat next to a priest. The man's tie was stained, his face was plastered with red lipstick, and a half empty bottle of gin was sticking out of his torn coat pocket. He opened his newspaper and began reading. After a few minutes, the disheveled man turned to the priest and asked, "Say, Father, what causes arthritis?"

The priest replied "Mister, it's caused by loose living, being with cheap women, too much alcohol and a contempt for your fellow man."

"Well I'll be," the drunk muttered, returning to his paper.

The priest, thinking about what he had said, nudged the man and apologized, "I'm very sorry. I didn't mean to come on so strong. How long have you had arthritis?"

"I don't have it Father. I was just reading here that the Pope does."

■

A guy is going down on his girlfriend and says, "Man you have a big pussy! Man you have a big pussy!"

She snaps back, "Why'd you say it twice?"

He replies, "I didn't..."

■

A young man was showing off his new sports car to his girlfriend. She was thrilled at the speed. "If I do 200mph, will you take off your clothes?" he asked.

"Yes!" said his adventurous girlfriend. And as he gets up to 200, she peeled off all her clothes. Unable to keep his eyes on the road, the car skidded onto some gravel and flipped over. The naked girl was thrown clear, but he was jammed beneath the steering wheel. "Go and get help!" he cried.

"But I can't. I'm naked and my clothes are gone!"

"Take my shoe", he said, "and cover yourself."

Holding the shoe over her pubes, the girl ran down the road and found a service station. Still holding the shoe between her legs, she pleaded to the service station proprietor, "Please help me! My boyfriend's stuck!"

The proprietor looked at the shoe and said, "There's nothing I can do...he's in too far."

■

A young man and his date were parked on a back road some distance from town. They were about to have sex when the girl stopped. "I really should have mentioned this earlier, but I'm actually a hooker and I charge $20 for sex."

The man reluctantly paid her, and they did their thing. After a cigarette, the man just sat in the driver's seat looking out the window.

"Why aren't we going anywhere?" asked the girl. "Well, I should have mentioned this before, but I'm actually a taxi driver, and the fare back to town is $25…"

■

A Male patient just recovered successfully from a sex threatening health attack. He was wearing an oxygen mask over his mouth and nose and laying on hospital bed. An young nurse came to cleanse his body with sponge.

The patient mumbled, "Are my testicles black?"

Nurse replied, "I don't know Sir, I am just setting you clean"

The patient repeated again, "Are my testicles black?"

Nurse was quite embarrassed to answer the question and said "Sir everything should be OK"

The patient just kept on asking again and again, "Are my testicles black?" Nurse could not bear a patient concerned so much. So she raised his gown, moved her hand to find and grab his penis and testicle, moved it all around, checked very closely and suddenly man ejaculated on nurse's hand.

The man pulls off his oxygen mask, embarrassed at the fiasco says loudly enough, "Ma'am, Thanks but I still need to know 'Are my tests results back?'"

■

Steve and his buddies were hanging out and planning an upcoming fishing trip. Unfortunately, he had to tell them that he couldn't go this time because his wife wouldn't let him. After a lot of teasing and name calling, Steve headed home frustrated. The following week when Steve's buddies arrived at the lake to set up camp, they were shocked to see Steve. He was already sitting at the campground with a cold beer, swag rolled out, fishing rod in hand, and a camp fire glowing.

"How did you talk your missus into letting you go Steve?"

"I didn't have to," Steve replied.

"Yesterday, when I left work, I went home and slumped down in my chair with a beer to drown my sorrows because I couldn't go fishing. Then the ol' lady Snuck up behind me and covered my eyes and said, 'Surprise'. When I peeled her hands back, she was standing there in a beautiful see through negligee and she said, 'Carry me into the bedroom, tie me to the bed and you can do whatever you want,' So, Here I am!"

■

A bus full of Nuns falls of a cliff and they all die. They arrive at the gates of heaven and meet St. Peter.

St. Peter says to them "Sisters, welcome to Heaven. In a moment I will let you all though the pearly gates, but before I may do that, I must ask each of you a single question. Please form a single-file line." And they do so.

St. Peter turns to the first Nun in the line and asks her "Sister, have you ever touched a penis?"

The Sister Responds "Well... there was this one time... that I kinda sorta... touched one with the tip of my pinky finger..."

St. Peter says "Alright Sister, now dip the tip of your pinky finger in the Holy Water, and you may be admitted." and she did so.

St. Peter now turns to the second nun and says "Sister, have you ever touched a penis?"

"Well.... There was this one time... that I held one for a moment..."

"Alright Sister, now just wash your hands in the Holy Water, and you may be admitted" and she does so. Now at this, there is a noise, a jostling in the line. It seems that one nun is trying to cut in front of another!

St. Peter sees this and asks the Nun "Sister Susan, what is this? There is no rush!"

Sister Susan responds "Well if I'm going to have to gargle this stuff, I'd rather do it before Sister Mary sticks her ass in it!"

■

A few days after Christmas, a mother was working in the kitchen listening to her young son playing with his new electric train in the living room.

She heard the train stop and her son said, "All of you sons of b*tches who want off, get the hell off now, cause this is the last stop! And all of you sons of b*tches who are getting on, get your asses in the train, cause we're going down the tracks."

The mother went nuts and told her son, "We don't use that kind of language in this house. Now I want you to go to your room and you are to stay there for TWO HOURS. When you come out, you may play with your train, but I want you to use nice language."

Two hours later, the son comes out of the bedroom and resumes playing with his train. Soon the train stopped and the mother heard her son say, "All passengers who are disembarking from the train, please remember to take all of your belongings with you. We thank you for riding with us today and hope your trip was a pleasant one. We hope you will ride with us again soon." She hears the little boy continue, "For those of you just boarding, we ask you to stow all of your hand luggage under your seat. Remember, there is no smoking on the train. We hope you will have a pleasant and relaxing journey with us today."

As the mother began to smile, the child added, "For those of you who are pissed off about the TWO HOUR delay, please see the b*tch in the kitchen."

■

A young guy from Nebraska moves to Florida and goes to a big "everything under one roof" department store looking for a job.

The Manager says, "Do you have any sales experience?"

The kid says, "Yeah. I was a salesman back in Omaha."

Well, the boss liked the kid and gave him the job. "You start tomorrow." I'll come down after we close and see how you did." His first day on the job was rough, but he got through it.

After the store was locked up, the boss came down. "How many customers bought something from you today?

The kid says, "One".

The boss says, "Just one? Our sales people average 20 to 30 customers a day. How much was the sale for?"

The kid says, "$101,237.65 ".

The boss says, "$101,237.65? What the heck did you sell?"

The kid says, "First, I sold him a small fish hook. Then I sold him a medium fishhook. Then I sold him a larger fishhook. Then I sold him a new fishing rod. Then I asked him where he was going fishing and he said down the coast, so I told him he was going to need a boat, so we went down to the boat department and I sold him a twin engine Boston Whaler. Then he said he didn't think his Honda Civic would pull it, so I took him down to the automotive department and sold him that 4x4 Expedition."

The boss said, "A guy came in here to buy a fish hook and you sold him a BOAT and a TRUCK?"

The kid said, "No, the guy came in here to buy Tampons for his wife, and I said, 'Dude, your weekend's shot, you should go fishing.'"

■

Three sisters decided to get married on the same day to save their parents the expense of separate weddings. As a further step to reduce the price tag, the three sisters resolved to spend their honeymoon night at home. Later that night, their mother couldn't sleep, so she went to the kitchen for a cup of tea. On her way, she tiptoed by her oldest daughter's bedroom and heard her screaming.

The mother thought to herself, "That's normal, especially on her wedding night."

She snuck by her second oldest daughter's room and heard her laughing. "That's normal too," she said, smiling to herself.

Finally, she slipped by her youngest daughter's room where she didn't hear a peep, but she thought nothing of it. The next morning in the kitchen, after the husbands had gone out, the woman asked her eldest daughter about last night's noises.

"Well Mom," she replied, "you always said if it hurt I should scream."

"You're absolutely right sweetheart, "the mother assured her, turning to her middle daughter.

"Now why were you laughing?" she asked. "You always said if it tickled, I could laugh," she answered. "True enough, honey."

The mother smiled, remembering her newlywed days. "Now it's your turn, baby," she said turning to her youngest daughter.

"Why was it so quiet in your room last night?"

"Mom, don't you remember? You always told me never to talk with my mouth full."

■

Jim decided to propose to Sandy, but prior to her acceptance. Sandy had to confess to her man about her childhood illness. She informed Jim that she suffered a disease that left her breasts at maturity of a 12 years old. He stated that it was OK because he loved her so much.

"I too have a problem. My penis is the same size as an infant and I hope you could deal with that once we are married."

She said, "Yes I will marry you and learn to live with your infant penis."

Sandy and Jim got married and they could not wait so Jim whisked Sandy off to their hotel suite and they started touch teasing, holding one another. As Sandy put her hands in Jim's pants, she began to scream and ran out of the room! Jim ran after her to find out what was wrong.

She said, "You told me your penis was the size of an infant!" "Yes it is: 8 pounds, 7 ounces, 19 inches long!"

■

Little Johnny comes down to breakfast. Since they live on a farm, his mother asks if he had done his chores.

"Not yet," said Little Johnny. His mother tells him no breakfast until he does his chores. Well, he's a little pissed off, so he goes to feed the chickens, and he kicks a chicken. He goes to feed the cows, and he kicks a cow. He goes to feed the pigs and he kicks a pig. He goes back in for breakfast and his mother gives him a bowl of dry cereal.

"How come I don't get any eggs and bacon? Why don't I have any milk in my cereal?" he asks.

"Well," his mother says, "I saw you kick a chicken, so you don't get any eggs for a week. I saw you kick the pig, so you don't get any bacon for a week either. I also saw you kick the cow, so for a week you aren't getting any milk."

Just then, his father comes down for breakfast and kicks the cat halfway across the kitchen. Little Johnny looks up at his mother with a smile, and says: "Are you going to tell him, or should I?"

■

A man escapes from prison where he has been for 15 years. He breaks into a house to look for money and guns and finds a young couple in bed. He orders the guy out of bed and ties him to a chair, while tying the girl to the bed he gets on top of her, kisses her neck, then gets up and goes into the bathroom. While he's in there, the husband tells his wife: "Listen, this guy's an escaped convict, look at his clothes! He probably spent lots of time in jail and hasn't seen a woman in years. I saw how he kissed your neck. If he wants s*x, don't resist, don't complain, do whatever he tells you. Satisfy him no matter how much he nauseates you. This guy is probably very dangerous. If he gets angry, he'll k*ll us. Be strong, honey. I love you."

To which his wife responds: "He wasn't kissing my neck. He was whispering in my ear. He told me he was gay, thought you were cute, and asked me if we had any vaseline. I told him it was in the bathroom. Be strong honey. I love you too!"

■

One night a little girl walks in on her parents having sex. The mother is going up and down on the father and when she sees her daughter looking at them she immediately stops.

"What are you doing, Mommy?"

The mother too embarassed to tell her little girl about sex so she makes up an answer.

"Well, sweetie, sometimes daddy's tummy gets too big so I have to jump up and down on it to flatten it out."

The little girl replies, "Well, mommy you really shouldn't bother with that."

The mother has a confused look on her face, "Why do you say that sweetheart?"

The little girl replies, "Because mommy, everytime you leave in the morning, the lady next door comes over and blows it back up."

■

Little Billy came home from school to see the families pet rooster dead in the front yard. Rigor mortis had set in and it was flat on its back with its legs in the air. When his Dad came home Billy said,

"Dad our roosters dead and his legs are sticking in the air. Why are his legs sticking in the air?"

His father thinking quickly said, "Son, that's so God can reach down from the clouds and lift the rooster straight up to heaven."

"Gee Dad that's great," said little Billy.

A few days later, when Dad came home from work, Billy rushed out to meet him yelling, "Dad, Dad we almost lost Mom today!"

"What do you mean?" said Dad. "Well Dad, I got home from school early today and went up to your bedroom and there was Mom flat on her back with her legs in the air screaming, "Jesus I'm coming, I'm coming" If it hadn't of been for Uncle George holding her down we'd have lost her for sure!"

■

The head nun tells the two new nuns that they have to paint their room without getting any paint on their clothes. So the one nun says to the other,

"Hey, let's take all our clothes off, fold them up, and lock the door."

So they do this, and begin painting their room. Soon they hear a knock at the door. They ask, "Who is it?"

"Blind man!" The nuns look at each other, then one nun says, "He's blind, he can't see. What could it hurt." They let him in. The blind man walks in and says,

"Hey, nice t*ts. Where do you want me to hang the blinds?"

■

A woman decided to have a face lift for her birthday. She spent $5000 and felt really good about the results. On her way home she stopped at a dress shop to look around. As she was leaving, she said to the sales clerk,

"I hope you don't mind me asking, but how old do you think I am?"

"About 35,"he replied.

"I'm actually 47," the woman said, feeling really happy. After that she went into McDonald's for lunch and asked the order taker the same question.

He replied, "Oh, you look about 29."

"I am actually 47!" she said, feeling really good. While standing at the bus stop she asked an old man the same question.

He replied, "I am 85 years old and my eyesight is going. But when I was young there was a sure way of telling a woman's age. If I put my hand up your skirt I will be able to tell your exact age." There was no one around, so the woman said,

"What the hell?" and let him slip his hand up her skirt. After feeling around for a while, the old man said,

"OK, You are 47."

Stunned, the woman said, "That was brilliant! How did you do that?"

The old man replied, "I was behind you in line at McDonald's."

■

A psychiatrist was conducting a group therapy session with three young mothers and their small children.

"You all have obsessions," he observed.

To the first mother, he said, "You are obsessed with eating. You've even named your daughter Candy."

He turned to the second mom. "Your obsession is money. Again, it manifests itself in your child's name, Penny."

At this point, the third mother got up, took her little boy by the hand and whispered, "Come on, Dick, let's go."

■

While watching TV with his wife, a man tosses peanuts into the air and catches them in his mouth. Just as he throws another peanut into the air, the front door opens, causing him to turn his head. The peanut falls into his ear and gets stuck. His daughter comes in with her date.

The man explains the situation, and the daughter's date says, "I can get the peanut out." He tells the father to sit down, shoves two fingers into the father's nose, and tells him to blow hard. The father blows, and the peanut flies out of his ear. After the daughter takes her date to the kitchen for something to eat, the mother turns to the father and says,

"Isn't he smart? I wonder what he plans to be."

The father says, "From the smell of his fingers, I'd say our son-in-law."

■

A dick has a sad life. His hair's a mess, his family is nuts, his neighbor's an asshole, his best friend's a pussy, and his owner beats him.

■

Harry and his wife are having hard financial times, so they decide that she'll become a hooker. She's not quite sure what to do, so Harry says,

"Stand in front of that bar and pick up a guy. Tell him that you charge a hundred bucks. If you got a question, I'll be parked around the corner."

She's standing there for 5 minutes when a guy pulls up and asks, "How much?"

She says, "A hundred dollars."

He says, "All I got is thirty".

She says, "Hold on," and runs back to Harry and asks, "What can he get for thirty?"

"A hand job", Harry reply. She runs back and tells the guy all he gets for thirty dollar is a hand job. He agrees. She gets in the car. He unzips his pants, and out pops this HUGE... She stares at it for a minute, and then says, "I'll be right back."

She runs back to Harry, and asks, "Can you loan this guy seventy bucks?"

■

A guy walks into a pub and sees a sign hanging over the bar that reads: CHEESEBURGER: $1.50 CHICKEN SANDWICH: $2.50 HAND JOB: $10.00.

He walks up to the bar and beckons one of the three exceptionally attractive blondes serving drinks. "Can I help you?" she asks.

"I was wondering," whispers the man. "Are you the one who gives the hand jobs?"

"Yes," she purrs. "I am."

The man replies, "Well, wash your hands. I want a cheeseburger."

■

A cowboy walks into a bar and takes a seat next to a very attractive woman. He gives her a quick glance then causally looks at his watch for a moment. The woman notices this and asks, "Is your date running late?"

"No", he replies," I just got this state-of the-art watch, and I was just testing it.."

The intrigued woman says, "A state-of-the-art watch? What's so special about it?"

41

The cowboy explains, "It uses alpha waves to talk to me telepathically."

The lady says, "What's it telling you now?"

"Well, it says you're not wearing any panties."

The woman giggles and replies "Well it must be broken because I am wearing panties!"

The cowboy smiles, taps his watch and says, "Damn thing's an hour fast."

■

A lady walks into a fancy jewellery store. She browses around, spots a beautiful diamond bracelet and walks over to inspect it. As she bends over to look more closely she inadvertently breaks wind. Very embarrassed, she looks around nervously to see if anyone has noticed her little accident and prays that a sales person doesn't pop up right now. As she turns around, her worst nightmare materializes in the form of a salesman standing right behind her. Cool as a cucumber and displaying complete professionalism, the salesman greets the lady with,

"Good day, Madam How may we help you today?" Very uncomfortably, but hoping that the salesman may not have been there at the time of her little "accident!" she asks,

"Sir, what is the price of this lovely bracelet?"

He answers, "Madam, if you farted just looking at it, you're going to shit when I tell you the price."

■

A girl realized that she had grown hair between her legs. She got worried and asked her mom about that hair. Her mom calmly said:

"That part where the hair has grown is called Monkey, be proud that your monkey has grown hair." the girl smiled.

At dinner, she told her sister: "My monkey has grown hair."

Her sister smiled and said: "That's nothing, mine is already eating bananas."

■

A farmer goes out and buys a new, young rooster. As soon as he brings him home, the young rooster rushes and screws all 150 of the farmers hens. The farmer is impressed. At lunchtime, the young rooster again screws all 150 hens. The farmer is not just impressed anymore, he is worried. Next morning, not only is the rooster screwing the hens but he is screwing the turkeys, ducks even the cow. Later farmer looks out into the barnyard and finds the rooster stretched out, limp as a rag, his eyes closed, dead and vultures circling overhead. The farmer runs out, looks down at the young roosters limp body and says: "You deserved it, you horny bastard!" And the young rooster opens one eye, points up at the vultures with his wing, and says, Shhhh!,they are about to land."

∎

Mr. Bear and Mr. Rabbit live in the same forest, but they don't like each other. One day, they come across a golden frog who offers them three wishes each. Mr. Bear wishes that all the other bears in the forest were female. Mr. Rabbit wishes for a crash helmet. Mr. Bear's second wish is that all the bears in the neighboring forests were female as well. Mr. Rabbit wishes for a motorcycle. Mr. Bear's final wish is that all the other bears in the world were female, leaving him the only male bear in the world. Mr. Rabbit revs the engine of his motorcycle and says, "I wish that Mr. Bear was gay!" and rides off.

∎

A man was shaving in the bathroom when all of a sudden bubba, the boy he pay to mow his lawn comes in to take a piss. Well, the man can't help but look over his shoulder and he is surprised, "bubba, what's your secret?"

Bubba says well, every night before I go to get in bed with a woman I whack my dick on the bedpost three times." So the man decides to try it that very night. So he got to bed and whacked his dick on the bedpost three times and the wife wakes up and says bubba, is that you?"

∎

A guy walks into the bar of a restaurant and goes to the bartender and asks "how much for a beer?"

The bartender replies "$1".

The customer completely amazed, orders a beer then asks the bartender "Well then how much for a NY sirloin, with side of mashed potatoes and salad, and an entire cheesecake for desert?"

The Bartender reply's "$5". The guy still amazed then orders everything and after he is done eating his meal then says "Wow, this place is amazing, I really wish I could meet the owner of this place".

The bartender then says "Oh well, he's upstairs in his office with my wife".

The guy looks all confused then asks "What is he doing upstairs in his office with your wife?"

The bartender then says "The same thing I'm doing to his business".

Guy: Wanna suck my dick?

Girl: No.

Guy: Probably for the best. I mean, it has a label-Warning! Choking Hazard!

Girl: Isn't that the warning put on tiny objects?

.

This beautiful woman one day walks into a doctor's office and the doctor is bowled over by how stunningly awesome she is. All his professionalism goes right out the window... He tells her to take her pants, she does, and he starts rubbing her thighs. "Do you know what I am doing?" asks the doctor?

"Yes, checking for abnormalities." she replies. He tells her to take off her shirt and bra, she takes them off. The doctor begins rubbing her breasts and asks, "Do you know what I am doing now?",

She replies, "Yes, checking for cancer." Finally, he tells her to take off her panties, lays her on the table, gets on top of her and starts having s*x with her. He says to her, "Do you know what I am doing now?"

She replies, "Yes, getting herpes – that's why I am here!"

.

The manager hired a new secretary. She was young, sweet and polite. One day while taking dictation, she noticed his fly was open. While leaving the room, she courteously said, "Oh, sir, did you know that your barracks door is open?" He did not understand her remark, but later on he happened to look down and saw that his zipper was open. He decided to have some fun with his new employee. Calling her in, he asked,

"By the way, Miss Jones, when you saw my barracks door open this morning, did you also see a soldier standing at attention?" The secretary, who was quite witty, replied,

"Why, no sir, all I saw was a little, disabled veteran, sitting on two duffel bags!"

.

Sex is like math: Add the bed Subtract the clothes, Divide the legs and pray you don't multiply.

.

I told my crush at school, "If you love me, come wearing red tomorrow." The next day she came in wearing black! When she dropped her pen and she bent over to pick it up, I got a look up her skirt at her red thong. Moral of the story: she really loves me underneath it all.

■

A guy was standing in a bar when a stranger walks in. After a while they get to talking and at about 10:30 PM the second guy says, "Oh well, I better get home. My wife doesn't like me to stay out during late night."

The first guy replies, "I'll help you out of this. Just do what I say. Go home. Sneak into the bedroom. Pull back the covers. Get down between her legs then lick, lick and lick for about 20 minutes and there will be no complaints in the morning."

The guy agrees to try that and continues drinking with him for two more hours before heading home to give it a try. When he got home, the house was pitch black. He sneaks upstairs into the bedroom, pulled back the covers and proceeded to lick for 20 minutes. The bed was like a swamp so he decided to wash his face. As he walked into the bathroom, his wife was sitting on the toilet. Seeing her he screamed,

"What the hell are you doing in here?!" "Quiet!", she exclaimed. "You'll wake my mother."

■

Boy in the bath with his mum.

Boy says, "What's that hairy thing mum ?"

Mum replies, "That is my sponge."

"Oh yes," says the boy, "The babysitters got one, I've seen her washing dads face with it ."

■

"Doc, I think my son has VD," a patient told his urologist on the phone, "The only woman he's screwed is our maid."

"Okay, don't be hard on him. He's just a kid," the medic soothed, "Get him in here right away and I'll take care of him."

"But I've been screwing the maid too, and I've got the same symptoms he has."

"Then you come in with him and I'll fix you both up," replied the doctor.

"Well," the man admitted, "I think my wife has it too." "Oh crap!" the physician roared, "That means we've all got it!"

■

I was in Venice Beach in January and there was a homeless man with a sign that said "1 dollar for dirty joke." Seemed like a good investment to me so I gladly handed over a dollar.

Homeless man: "Alright sir what's your name?"

Me: "John"

Homeless man: "So Johnny, there is black rooster alright? How many legs does that chicken have."

Me: "Two?"

Homeless man: "Right, now how many wings this black rooster got?"

Me: "Two?"

Homeless man: "Right, now how many eyes this black rooster got?"

Me: "Two?"

Homeless man: "Right again, now there is this white cat walking around how many hairs are on that white cat?"

Me: "I don't know? A lot?"

Homeless man: "Well Johnny, why do you know so much about black cock and not enough about white pussy."

■

Sixth grade science teacher Mrs. Samson asks her class: "Who can tell me which organ of the human body expands to 10 times its usual size when stimulated?" Nobody raises a hand, so she calls on the first student to look her way.

"Mary, can you tell me which organ of the human body expands to 10 times its usual size when stimulated?"

Mary stands up, blushing furiously. "How dare you ask such a question?" she says. "I'm going to complain to my parents, who will complain to the principal, who will have you fired!"

Mrs. Sampson is shocked by Mary's reaction, but undaunted. She asks the class the question again, and this time Sam raises his hand. "Yes, Sam?" says Mrs. Sampson.

"Ma'am, the correct answer is the iris of the human eye."

"Very good, Sam. Thank you." Mrs. Sampson then turns to Mary and says, "Mary, I have 3 things to tell you: first, it's clear that you have not done your homework. Second, you have a dirty mind. And third, I fear one day you are going to be sadly disappointed."

■

A man suffered a serious heart attack while shopping in a store. The store clerk called 911 when they saw him collapse to the floor. The paramedics rushed the man to the nearest hospital where he had emergency open heart bypass surgery. He awakened from the surgery to find himself in the care of nuns at the Catholic Hospital. A nun was seated next to his bed holding a clipboard loaded with several forms, and a pen. She asked him how he was going to pay for his treatment.

"Do you have health insurance?" she asked.

He replied in a raspy voice, "No health insurance."

The nun asked, "Do you have money in the bank?"

He replied, "No money in the bank."

"Do you have a relative who could help you with the payments?" asked the irritated nun.

He said, "I only have a spinster sister, and she is a nun."

The nun became agitated and announced loudly, "Nuns are not spinsters! Nuns are married to God."

The patient replied, "Perfect. Send the bill to my brother-in-law."

■

Joe is on his last day at work as a mailman. He receives many thank-you cards and monetary gifts along his route. When he gets to the very last house, he is greeted by a gorgeous housewife, who invites him in for lunch. Joe happily accepts. After lunch, the woman invites him up to the bedroom for some "desert." Joe happily accepts again. When they are done, the woman gives him a dollar. Joe asks what the dollar is all about.

The woman replies: "It was my husband's suggestion. When I told him that it was your last day at work, he told me 'F**k him, give him a dollar. The lunch was my idea."

■

A woman walks into her accountant's office and tells him that she needs to file her taxes. The accountant says, "Before we begin, I'll need to ask a few questions." He gets her name, address, social security number, etc. and then asks, "What is your occupation?"

The woman replies, "I'm a whore."

The accountant balks and says, "No, no, no. That will never work. That is much too crass. Let's try to rephrase that."

The woman, "Ok, I'm a prostitute."

"No, that is still too crude. Try again."

They both think for a minute, then the woman states, "I'm a chicken farmer."

47

The accountant asks, "What does chicken farming have to do with being a whore or a prostitute?"

"Well, I raised over 5,000 cocks last year."

■

A hunter goes into the woods to hunt a bear. He carries his trusty 22-gauge rifle with him. After a while, he spots a very large bear, takes aim, and fires. When the smoke clears, the bear is gone.

A moment later, the bear taps the hunter on the shoulder and says, "No one shoots at me and gets away with it. You have two choices: I can rip your throat out and eat you, or you can drop your trousers, bend over, and I'll f**k you." The hunter decides that anything is better than death, so he drops his trousers and bends over; and the bear does what he said he would do. After the bear has left, the hunter pulls up his trousers and staggers back into town. He's pretty mad. He buys a much larger gun and returns to the forest. He sees the same bear, aims, and fires. When the smoke clears, the bear is gone. A moment later the bear taps the hunter on the shoulder and says,

"You know what to do." Afterward, the hunter pulls up his trousers, crawls back into town, and buys a bazooka. Now he's really mad. He returns to the forest, sees the bear, aims, and fires. The force of the bazooka blast knocks him flat on his back. When the smoke clears, the bear is standing over him and says,

"You're not doing this for the hunting, are you?"

■

A young punk gets on the cross-town bus. He's got spiked, multi-colored hair that's green, purple, and orange. His clothes are a tattered mix of leather rags. His legs are bare and he's wearing worn-out shoes. His entire face and body are riddled with pierced jewelry and his earrings are big, bright feathers. He sits down in the only vacant seat that's directly across from an old man who glares at him for the next ten miles. Finally, the punk gets self-conscious and barks at the old man,

"What are you looking at you old fart... didn't you ever do anything wild when you were young?"

Without missing a beat, the old man replies, "Yeah, back when I was young and in the Navy, I got really drunk one night in Singapore and screwed a parrot.... I thought maybe you were my son."

■

Man goes to a fancy dress party wearing only a glass jar on his p*nis.

Lady asks, "What are you?"

He says, "I'm a fireman."

"But you're only wearing a glass jar," says the woman.

He says, "Exactly, in an emergency, break glass." Pull knob and I'll cum as fast as I can!".

■

A man took his pregnant wife to the hospital. The doctor looked her over and told them it would be a rather difficult delivery. He offered to let the couple try an experimental procedure. The woman would be connected to a machine that would transfer part of the pain to the father of the baby, thus reducing her own. The man quickly agreed. The doctor warned him, though, that there was a slight bug in the machine that caused it to amplify the pain sent to the father by ten times, and if the pain became too much for to bear would he please let the doctor know. The doctor turned on the machine and watched the man. The man said he felt absolutely fine and he could take more. The doctor turned the dial up to 40, 60, 80, and finally 100% of the pain, times ten. The woman delivered the baby painlessly and the doctor stared at the man, astonished at how he could not even flinch with that much pain brought upon him. The couple took the new baby home. There, on the front step, the mailman lay dead.

■

A teenage girl come home from school and asks her mother, "Is it true what Rita just told me?"

"What's that?" asks her mother.

"That babies come out of the same place where boys put their penises?" said her daughter.

"Yes it is dear!" replies her mother, pleased that the subject had finally come up and that she wouldn't have to explain it to her daughter.

"But then, when I have a baby," responded the teenager, "won't it knock my teeth out?"

■

A boy watches his mum and dad having s*x he ask, "What are you doing ?"

His dad replies, "Making you a brother or sister!" Boy say, "Do her d*ggy style I want a puppy."

■

A little boy came home from school and his homework assignment was to find out what the difference was between hypothetically and realistically, so he asked his dad.

His dad said, "Well, go ask your mom if she would sleep with the mail man for $1,000,000."

He went and asked and came back and said, "She said yes".

"Well", said the dad, "Go ask your sister the same question."

He did and came back and said, "She said yes."

And the dad said, "Now go ask your brother the same thing."

He did and came back and said, "He said yes too!"

And the dad said, "Well hypothetically we're sitting on three million dollars, realistically we're living with 2 whores and a fag!".

■

Girl: Baby I'm wet.

Boy: Want a paper towel?

Girl: No, I want more then that,

Boy: Want 2 paper towels?

Girl: No, baby I want something big and round,

Boy: Damn you want the whole roll?